Those Were The Days

OrangeBooks Publication

1st Floor, Rajhans Arcade, Mall Road, Kohka, Bhilai, Chhattisgarh 490020

Website: **www.orangebooks.in**

© Copyright, 2024, Author

All rights reserved. No part of this book may be reproduced, stored in a retrieval system, or transmitted, in any form by any means, electronic, mechanical, magnetic, optical, chemical, manual, photocopying, recording or otherwise, without the prior written consent of its writer.

First Edition, 2024

ISBN: 978-93-5621-852-9

Those Were The Days

IIT AND OTHER POEMS

VINOD KHURANA

OrangeBooks Publication
www.orangebooks.in

Contents

1. Those Were The Days 1
2. Three Decades 4
3. Happy Birthday 6
4. Host 8
5. Break The Silence 10
6. Upside Down 12
7. Making Us Humans 14
8. A Child Saint 15
9. Presence of Mind 17
10. Squeak 19
11. The Language of Love 21
12. Poke 24
13. Yoga and Wine 25
14. Happy Dussehra 27
15. Moderation 29
16. Say it in One Word 31
17. Jacuzzi or A Tubewell Pond 33

18. What it Was	35
19. Why Innocent People Plead Guilty	38
20. Slang We Used At IIT	40
21. Friendship	42
22. A Letter to Oneself	45
23. A Journey to Watch	47
24. Awaiting New Year	49
25. More on New Year	52
26. A Chai Cup	54
27. Dusk and Dawn	56
28. Laughter	58
29. One Must Move On	60
30. What is Our Future	62
31. Light and Dark	64
32. Fight For Peace	66
33. Revisit The Past	68
34. Grace	70
35. Lost in The Woods	72
36. Old Age	75
37. Meaningful Goals	77
38. To Close The Distance	78
39. Silence and Speech	80
40. Childhood and Old Age	81

41. What We Hear and See	83
42. What Happens	85
43. Do or Die	87
44. Friends or Family	89
45. Those Early Days	91
46. To Run After Things	93
47. What's Worship	94
48. Home	96
49. Song of Nature	98
50. Blind Faith	100
51. Not Someone Else	102
52. To Be Watchful	103
53. Gift of Love	104
54. Battlefield of Mind	105
55. Make Me Whatever	106
56. My Dream	108
57. Cry For Help	110
58. Help Yourself	111
59. Sing A Song	112
60. Thoughts	114
61. Sow Such Deeds	116
62. Imagination	117
63. Nakedness	118

64. A Thief	120
65. Introspection	122
66. Change The Change	123
67. Prince of Hearts	125
68. Hope	127
69. Politics	129
70. Walls Hear	131
71. Why Sell Everything	133
72. House on Fire	135
73. Thorns and Friends	138
74. A House Divided	140

Those Were The Days

Sweet sixteen or seventeen
with a little beard growing,
lined up only in underwear
and that too dropping,
bend forward and then backward
the doctor said,
but what was he viewing!

And then followed ragging
which took away the shame
whatever little of it had remained,
those were the days of
induction and its ways.

And then began the grind
that was largely above the mind,
wish one could throw away the books
out of the window of one's room
and run away from there.

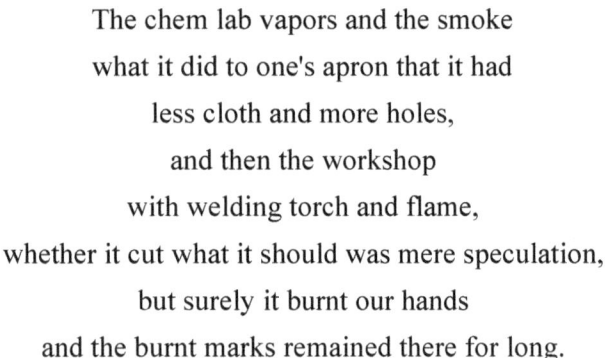

The chem lab vapors and the smoke
what it did to one's apron that it had
less cloth and more holes,
and then the workshop
with welding torch and flame,
whether it cut what it should was mere speculation,
but surely it burnt our hands
and the burnt marks remained there for long.

And then came the smithy
with hot iron and hammer,
what was to be given shape
it flew far away.

Those were the days
when fluid and quantum mechanics
tortured us in menacing ways,
but as time passed
the grind made us strong.

Those were the days

When the project work was done
one feared how to face the
viva voce and answer the questions
that were fired at us mercilessly.

Thankfully that too was cleared
and IIT graduates we did become,

Then came jobs and interviews
which made us travel all over the globe.

Each one accomplished
whatever one could,
and then came retirement
and self employment
but there was nothing to beat
what to us the IIT did,
those were the days
which we recollect time and again.

And when we meet
whenever possible,
we feel young again.

Vinod Khurana

Three Decades

In the three decades
from graduation to building up our career
brick by brick,
there's much that had happened.

We met as and when we could
but did not know then that we would later form
a more cohesive group.

The group became more vibrant
day after day.
But the experiences of everyone have further
enriched the group.

Those were the days

As you all know this group has become our lifeline,
and we want to keep it ever young and fine.

You'll agree that as's the group so are we,
so let's make the group the best it can ever be.

The whole life of the group we may fully live.
Long live the group and not a single day we
may miss.

Vinod Khurana

Happy Birthday

This day's special
brighter than ever before,
uncork a champagne
we would celebrate at home.

Gulla our darling
in time we all grow,
but we pray and wish
you grow younger every year.

Best of everything
be at your door,
liveliness and style
in you we adore.

Those were the days

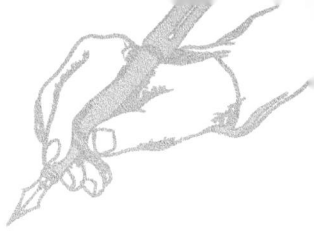

You defy everything
that fits into a mold,
each day's new
and newer wings you grow.

Life's to be lived
with no regret and no remorse,
each birthday be special
more memorable than before.

Happy Birthday to you
celebrate it to the full,
everything else can wait
our best wishes are always with you!

Host

Gill the host
wherever he goes
such fragrance he brings
which none can miss.

Time for reunion
and to sing
sweet melodies
with pop and swing.

While you drink
wines old and rich
drink one for us too
and spare time for a thought.

Those were the days

Though we may be far from you
but are far closer in our hearts,
we remember you a lot
in prayer and our thoughts.

We are but one
and each's its part
playing his role well
right from the start.

How quickly the time flies
yesterday it was a class,
now everyone a king of his pride
yet together we're still a bunch of nomads!

Vinod Khurana

Break The Silence

We all open the mailbox everyday
to get in touch with each other,
this getting together in virtual world
gives us a high in the real world.

Some of us let us know what they feel,
and some find no time to tell their story,
but that we are joined together
that matters and shall always will.

Those were the days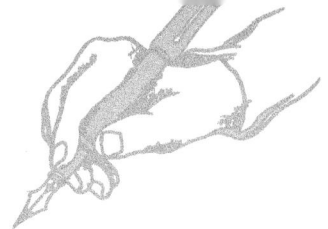

But silence too often
makes strangers of friends,
let us share what we can
each and all.

It's no small thing
that we have come so far,
and with each passing day
stronger becomes this bond!

Upside Down

She sees things upside down,
Not on their legs, but hanging down.

It is not her fault, just give it a thought,
A world on its head, down and out.

Land and waters above her head,
And the sky is laid beneath her feet.

Who holds and keeps her well in sight,
That she floats with steps so very light.

North's south and west's east,
Nothing makes sense wherever it is.

But the sun shall rise wherever it will.

Those were the days

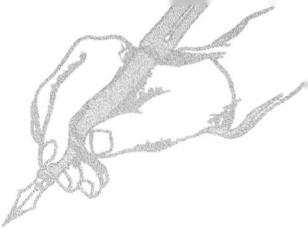

God has made her this way as a hint.

She walks backwards which you leave behind,
and where you stop, from there she begins.

When you rest, she hurries in speed,
With eyes open so lightly she sleeps.

She's made different, but special she's,
The world's in doldrums, wherever she sees.

On edge she lives, but after all a human she's
And wonders what will happen to the world as it's

She has to be assured from time to time,
For as yet, the time's not on her side.

The things should not be as they have been,
And the world shall sooner be seeing what with her eyes
she now sees.

Vinod Khurana

Making Us Humans

The land that made me me
and thee thee,
It still makes one we
and what we have not been.

A skirt may not cover what it must,
But small becomes big in a wink,
Lucky are the ones
Who wooed you as teens.

Small and hesitant they were then,
Now grown much confident and worthy beings.

The land that made us us,
Is now making them humans as best
as they could ever be!

Those were the days

A Child Saint

A child of three
brush in hand,
colours and paint
what a world he creates.

Who guides his hand
and gives him his thoughts,
with such a wonderful world view
which even the wise can't comprehend.

He's such an artist
in whom the divine works
Through and through,
Eyes innocent, with understanding so deep.

He creates in quick succession
in a great hurry, for He waits for him at the door,
to take him along, where's His throne,

From there he came, and with Him returns to his home.

A total of seven years in all
when childhood is still raw,
His wisdom and works could not be compared
Even with the best in the world.

A child saint extraordinary he was and the world
watched him in awe.

Those were the days

Presence of Mind

A cub I am
See what can I do
As I play and make fun
With danger lurking close

Fear strikes me too
But I don't freeze
My mind is alert
And my moves swift

When choice is limited
Between life and death
A child is no less
Who is fearless

Why instill much fear
That I shiver and cry
And give up soon
Without any fight

Vinod Khurana

When left with no option
Better fight to the finish
Or if it were possible
Make a calculated retreat

One wins in the battlefield
Another falls but bravely
He is also no less a hero
Who escapes daringly

Knowledge and wisdom mark a sage
But first he has to ensure his security
For which he needs presence of mind
And a childlike agility!

Those were the days

Squeak

Wherever you are, just squeak
So that we know where you have been
Or just post a few words
May be one, two or three

Long silence when it intervenes
Our faces go long and worrying deep
When we hear your footsteps
We know all is well, as it should be

We are no herd, no sheep
Yet we move together
In thick and thin
More it lasts, the better it is

Vinod Khurana

If one is away
Or gone his own way
We search him out
And then celebrate

Thus far we have come
Teens to nearly six decades
We shall stay put
Till His hand takes us away

Squeak or shout
Play and make sound
We are still together
Let's sing and laugh aloud !

Those were the days

The Language of Love

King of the jungle
And head of my pride
None can stand before me
I know no fear or fright.

But years before I was a child
Caged and sold for a few pice
Neither could I raise my voice
Nor I could fight.

My master took pity
Raising me like his own child
As I grew my nature showed off
Ferocious and wild.

He let me loose
In a jungle thick and wild
To mingle among my own
And like a king to live my life

A lion is a lion
Who rules as
per whims
I was no different
But something I missed.

My master in my thoughts
With such a big heart
Who taught me to love
To a lion, my God!

Those were the days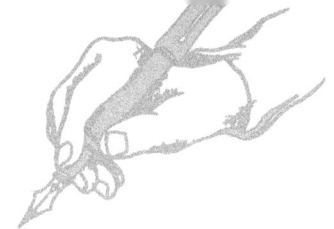

One day on prowl
When I saw my master
My joy knew no bounds
I jumped and danced all about.

A child I became
Whom he had so lovingly raised
And kissed him and licked him
In a warm embrace

An animal is an animal, no human
But he too feels and understands
The language of love is such
That every creature can fully understand.

Poke

What was once the pride of man
It hides itself in pain and shame
Why should it pay any tax when it's used
As an antique in showcase let it remain

Tongue, finger or nose can poke
But for me it is strictly no no
Who shall now explore the worlds
That crave and die for its very touch

A hermit they have made of man
Who regaled the world with its span
Poke or no poke it has become a joke
What once was the pride of man

The world is barren unless its pride is restored
And when it works what bliss is in its poke!

Those were the days

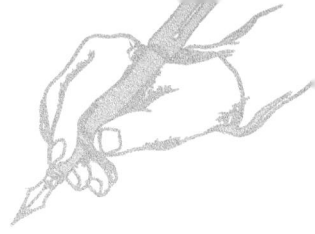

Yoga and Wine

Bend, stretch and tilt
No circus but a drill
It's yoga that I teach

A glass of wine to drink
To lift my mind and spirit
I write what I dare to think

Yoga teaches one discipline
To live life of a hermit
Without taste of any good thing

I bless all with every sip
And the drink for company
It makes my life so fulfilling

Do yoga day and night
And feel agile and light
But never indulge in any vice

Drink in style day and night
Entertain much but with no malice
Do no harm for there is no other vice

Yoga is revered far and wide
I bid goodbye healthy and ripe
A trail of light I leave behind

I lived in the hearts and minds
Lasting longer with a glass by my side
A trail of mirth and laughter I leave behind

One is the gift of east to mankind
The other in the west its very life
Woo either or both but do something worthwhile!

Those were the days

Happy Dussehra

The tussle between good and evil goes on
Goodness suffers but holds long
Evil rules but meets a bitter fall

As evil in human form lay sprawled
It spake thus as witnessed by the Lord
I wasn't right and committed wrong after wrong

I am still breathing but my last
Pray if You shall forgive me my past
None should emulate me but what I was not

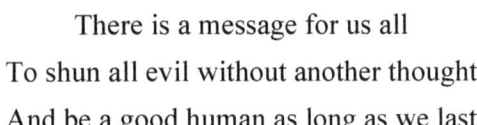

There is a message for us all
To shun all evil without another thought
And be a good human as long as we last

Time has come to celebrate after all
Good wins and evil falls
Ma blesses one and all

Happy Dussehra brings joy in our hearts
Vijay Dashmi greets you all
Shubham Bijoy say one and all

Those were the days

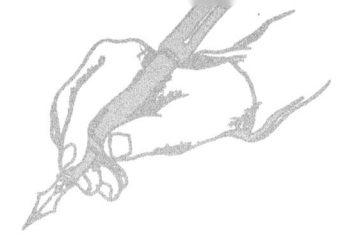

Moderation

It was his age
Dash and craze
Much merry did he make
A peg too many did he take.

His daily doze it became
A habit with its take
Somewhat he strayed
But no one to blame.

Living beyond ninety
A century he could have made
Had he lived like a hermit
With not a drop to taste.

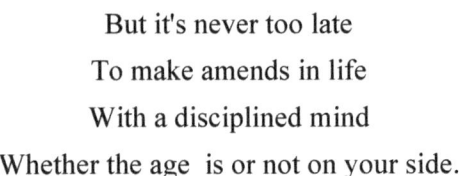

But it's never too late
To make amends in life
With a disciplined mind
Whether the age is or not on your side.

Moderation is the key
That unlocks the secrets
Taste all good things in life
Nothing untouched let there be.

It's is all in the age
Bubbling youth and its rage
Merry one should make
But leave a little for the old age!

Those were the days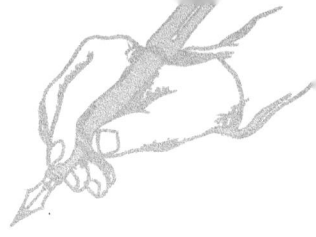

Say it in One Word

When silence falls short
One word says it all
More is noise
No music no ball.

No frills no drills
No glass no bash
Hold hand that warms
And love says it all.

No crown no frown
Splash and rain dance
What joy it gives
Our looks say it all.

When kids are at play
How merry they make
Kidding heals the sick
As no medicine will.

Two is good company
Let it long last
One who is left alone
How sad is his heart.

Hand and feet
They matter a lot
But brave never stop
With handicap or not.

When words fall short
Riches come to naught
Something inside talks
Hear and you know it all!

Those were the days

Jacuzzi or A Tubewell Pond

No sumo wrestlers
No brothers no twins
It's their own field
And they are pals thick.

They are no brats
Not young anymore
But age matters not
When spirit is young.

They drink and bathe
At the tube well that irrigates
While one takes a dip
The other patiently waits.

On the rim of the well is the bar
Two glasses and a bottle large
Peg after peg they gulp down
Neat and neck deep in the bath.

The crops in the field multiply
As they discuss and contemplate
The two wise men so engrossed
At what has and what may come to pass.

No sumo wrestlers
But pals thick
Their riches multiply
As they bathe and drink!

Those were the days

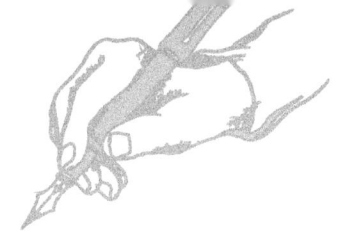

What it Was

Naked we stood
Like dumb fools
Whatever they do
We had to stand cool.

The doctor examined closely
Attendant stared
They nodded in agreement
And we were cleared.

It was a strange world
Of sharks and wolves
Who pounced on us
A bait sumptuous.

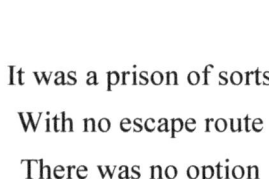

It was a prison of sorts
With no escape route
There was no option
But to reconcile soon.

What happened thereafter
It's an open book
No need to repeat
It is known and understood.

We were grilled and bullied
Ground and polished
The ordeal we survived
It was no ordinary thing.

Those were the days

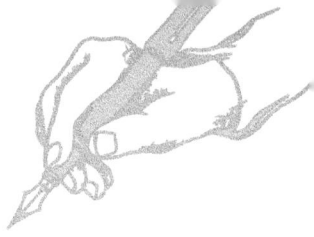

We who were lambs
Midway changed track
Some became wolves
And some sharks too.

It was a jungle indeed
Unfit for meek and weak
The grind we went through
It made us something.

It was what it was
But it gave us such confidence
That we could face the world
And its sharks and wolves!

Vinod Khurana

Why Innocent People Plead Guilty

Where justice is a bargain
And dirt cheap to platefuls
Innocents fear the law
And clean slates are at loss.

Law is blind but it sees
It's fair irrespective of verdict
But how the guilty goes scot free
And an innocent is behind bars.

Blame not the law
Blame not the system
But the culture of statistic
Where numbers find precedence over justice.

Those were the days

Guilty may go unpunished
But an innocent should never be punished
Charge not an innocent
And ask him to prove his innocence.

Where justice is a bargain
Judge and jury watch
Law becomes subordinate
When plea has sanctity of law!

Vinod Khurana

Slang We Used At IIT

We added to our vocabulary
Word by word
As a child with alphabet does

It was raw it was sharp
Nothing less stirred us
To shoot back or retort

Not in whispers
But loud and clear
Music so rustic it was

Sometimes it embarrassed
When volleys were exchanged left and right
And a guest or parent dropped

Those were the days

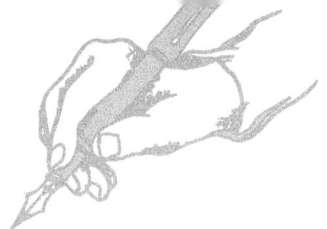

But they understood
The pressure we went through
We buckled not but faced it as a don

It brought us closer
These pet names and cuss words
When life was hard and unbearable

In retrospect when we think
It was the need of the time
That helped us to hold on and make a mark in our life!

Friendship

We come alone
And go alone
But we make friends
While we roam.

Brothers and sisters
By blood or creed
One who understands
He is a friend indeed.

A friend takes care
And is a well wisher
He expects nothing in return
Not even a good word.

Those were the days

He is no lover
But is close to you
And not so close
To witness your shortcomings.

He keeps proper distance
And gives enough space
But he will not walk away
And become a stranger again.

He likes your presence
And you like his nearness
When together they meet
They feel happy and upbeat.

Life has its ups and downs
But friendship helps maintain level
When heavy is the burden on your shoulder
It readily lends its own shoulder.

Expect not a favour from a friend
And embarrass him unnecessarily
He knows your need and will do for you
Not as a favour but for sake of friendship.

Free and uninhibited one feels
Such is the mark of good friendship
It remains intact as it is
When all the rest is reduced to nothing.

As we age and contemplate
We acknowledge with gratefulness
That the best that ever was in life
It was because of friends who stood by your side.

Spring and autumn are temporary
They are seasons that come and go
But the fragrance of friendship
Like an eternal spring it flows!

Those were the days

A Letter to Oneself

I write when you dominate the mind
And erase all which I write
For nothing comes right

I pause to think
To do something about it
Write a letter to none but me

I write but it's not what I want
Subtle, gross ,gentle or sharp
Because over my shoulder you watch

You are ever in my thoughts
My ego, my pride, my mind
And influence what I write

Vinod Khurana

I am uncomfortable with the thoughts
That mark your presence in whatever form
You are close but my words need privacy alone

I exclude you from my thoughts
And close my eyes wherever you are
To write all that I want

I write things which I kept from me
Exposing myself unpardonably
When buried they had troubled me so deeply

I write to myself all that I could
Which I couldn't have done mindfully
To reveal me to myself completely and truthfully!

Those were the days

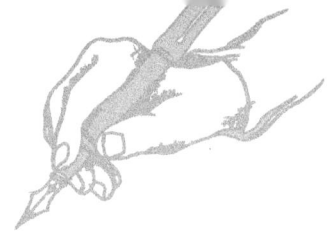

A Journey to Watch

A journey of thousand miles
It begins with a step
Waters flow thousands of miles
And meet the sea at its doorstep.

A step one has to take
And walk without break
Those who aim big
They don't rest on the way.

A child learns to walk
When first step she takes
No need to lose heart
With each step you gain.

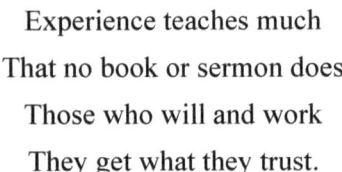

Experience teaches much
That no book or sermon does
Those who will and work
They get what they trust.

One who is inspired
He walks sure and firm
Setting his sight higher
He plucks the stars above.

The hills beckon from afar
The breeze across the seven seas
makes a melodious symphony
To welcome one and all.

They are on the march
Characters to watch
The show is set to begin
Come and play your part!

Those were the days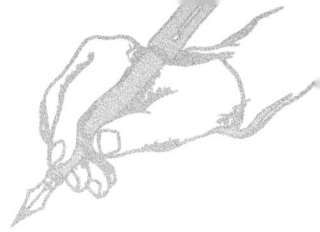

Awaiting New Year

A stranger there
but a lion at home
Rosy what was from distance
it's not so from close.

One who ruled the pride
became just a slave
Lost his native edge too
and aped strange manners and ways.

What one wills
that he does
But when will becomes a monkey
it can only wag its tail.

Things remained same
with negligible gain
Unfamiliar made style
and familiar appeared stale.

Then came the churning
The change that changed
the rules of the game
and then nothing remained the same.

Will became willing
strong and steely
Action became one's religion
and unity one's creed.

The home which was left behind
it regained its charm
What it now made
the world watched in awe.

Those were the days

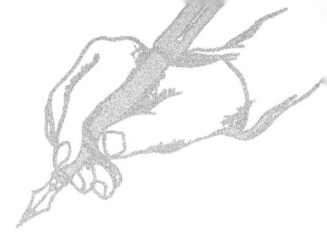

It's just a beginning
fresh and promising
It's strength's multiplying
and also its capability.

The glorious past which it had
it has raised its head again
History repeats itself
and it's now being rewritten once again.

Each day counts
The new year waits
Do all that one can
To make it great.

No longer now a stranger
he's back home
The new year now comes
with much more promise and hope!

Vinod Khurana

More on New Year

Newness is everywhere
Past is left behind
Together we go forward
Into the happier times.

No divisions of any kind
Doubts are left behind
Love bubbling in our hearts
And hope is our guide.

We did what we could
Now bigger are our dreams
We shall not let anything
To come in between.

There is no fear in our mind
And terror we shall extinguish
The hand of friendship we extend
And harbour no ill will.

Those were the days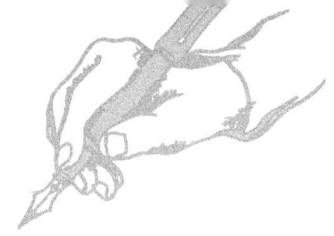

The world comes closer
And space we conquer
What appeared invincible
That now becomes doable.

Will and enterprise outshine
We leap and cover new grounds
The new year and its challenges
We woo with much hope and pride.

History writes a new chapter
Dazzling things happen
Preparations are in full swing
A brighter future is unfolding.

Come let us sing a new tune
Which was never heard before
And create with our zeal and labour
A new world never visualized before.

A Chai Cup

It's a chai cup
What colour and taste
To soothe your nerves
And to entertain.

It is my colour box
With tea bag I paint
Mind to visualize
And eye for detail.

Both go together
Chai and paint
One for living
The other to create.

Those were the days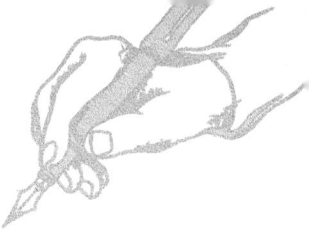

Paint is my passion
Hope I get a break
The artist in me
May not suffocate.

Gifted are many
Who have no penny
They can enrich the world
If you hold their hand and pull them up!

Vinod Khurana

Dusk and Dawn

Dusk lingers long
Terror is a blot
Intolerance is on the rise
And divided are the hearts.

Muster courage
Pull up the socks
Dusk is not for ever
There comes the dawn.

The new year beckons
It brings a new dawn
Wait a little more
With hope and confidence.

Every day is not the same
Sometime you lose
And sometime gain
It's all in the game.

Those were the days

Dusk and dawn
Light and darkness
They are like ups and downs
That challenge man to outdo and shine.

Whatever it has been
Let's us be doubly sure
We shall not fritter away
What comes with much hope.

Let's step into the new year
With no baggage of the past
But light and fresh as spring
And a spirit that knows no halt.

There is a lot we can do
And still more we shall do
To make the new year
Happier and prosperous too!

Laughter

Laugh morning evening
Or whenever you want
But stop
If one takes it to heart.

Things that don't straighten out
Or have no head or foot
Laugh them off
And feel light at heart.

See a child and what he does
He smiles and laughs most of the time
That's the natural instinct
With which we were born.

Those were the days

Where it goes as we grow
The smile on our face
And laughter that shakes
Farther we go from our natural state.

Discover the child in you
Put away the unnecessary seriousness
Bring back the bubbling freshness
With the laughter of a child in you!

Vinod Khurana

One Must Move On

Welcome home
in every heart you stay.
what it was
but irony of fate.

The clouds have passed
the sun is the same
bright and warm
the light is the same.

It's not easy to forget
and none can explain
but it's better to forgive them
who inflict the pain.

Those were the days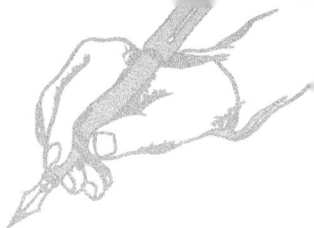

One must move on
and ride a fresh wave
life is ever flowing
with no pause or break.

Mistakes we make each and every day
innocently and in good faith
none is perfect and we learn this way
lifeless are the things that make no mistakes!

Vinod Khurana

What is Our Future

We are poached and killed
for pleasure and meat
there's retribution in nature
and none is spared in the least.

Yet you go about unconcerned
what has happened to thee
a child of nature you were
with a compassionate streak.

Law unto yourself
that's what you think
a jolt when it comes
on the face shall fall thee.

Those were the days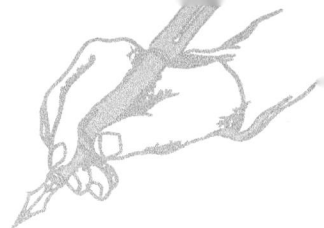

None will lift you
and none shall save thee
who pity not an innocent life
none shall pity thee.

What is our future
it may not trouble thee
but what future holds for you
we shudder to think!

Light and Dark

One begins where the other ends
day and night are like that
at dawn and dusk they meet
where they coexist.

Not as black and white
but in continuum
mixing and merging
with no beginning no end.

Life is not one or the other
but the two weaved together
one is at loss how to cross
this maze of light and dark.

Those were the days

White has all the colors we know
but in darkness there is none
yet it fills everything that exists
the moment light makes its exit.

Let us understand that both make sense
the brightness as well as darkness
the dark clouds have a silver lining
and life exists because sun sets and rises.

Fight For Peace

Why raise controversy
where there's none
when peace no one loves
there's only fight and chaos.

May be that's the way
to be counted anyway
who choose to live in peace
go unnoticed all the way.

Live whatever way one wants
but difference one should make
what use's that wisdom
unused that remains.

Those were the days

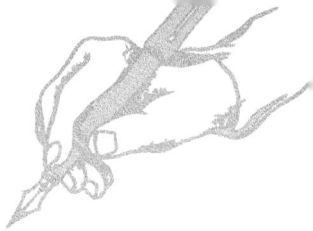

One can't fight with peace
but one can still find peace
even in a battlefield
righteous when one's.

When wrong's being done
how can one watch in peace
that fight is justified
which brings meaningful peace!

Vinod Khurana

Revisit The Past

Let bygone be bygone
but revisit it at times
to look at it differently
with passage of time.

Healing comes with wisdom
and wisdom with time
how can one be at peace
in the thick of time.

So move on and not be stuck in time
lest time passes and you are left behind.

Those were the days

What's past hold it not
or it holds you and leaves you not
free yourself from its clutches
however much you struggle with the past.

The past was yours
and you its part
it defines truly
how you evolved
revisit it at times
but with a grateful heart!

Grace

Nothing one brings
nothing one takes
life one lives
by his grace.

Do such acts
as abound in grace
and when one leaves
no regret remains.

Life is one beginning
and death no dead end
but just a diversion
towards a new end.

Those were the days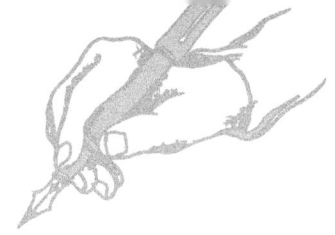

One does nothing
but what is willed
and when one kills
is that also willed.

How do we know
right from wrong
with our limited vision
and what we know not.

Desire nothing
but be alert and active
each breath matters
to life that thrives.

Understand everyone and everything
with a pure heart and unbiased mind
that's the wisdom contained in nutshell
in all the scriptures combined!

Vinod Khurana

Lost in The Woods

Silence that frightens
in the woods deep and dark
anything could happen
one may live or not.

Cross country she ran
through the green forests
but lost herself midway
it was time for sunset.

Tired and exhausted
she would have given up
but a faint hope flickered
that she may be discovered.

Those were the days

Her thoughts went back
to her family and little one
who needed breast feed
and her mom to soothe her.

The night fell
and darkness too
it poured heavily
and it was windy too.

Shivering terribly
and with her bare hands
the earth she dug deep
to protect herself from cold.

She lowered herself
into the hole that she had dug
and with some dust over her
she covered herself.

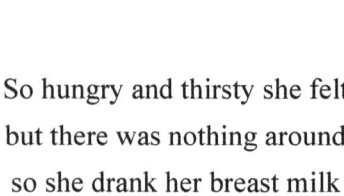

So hungry and thirsty she felt
but there was nothing around
so she drank her breast milk
which belonged to her baby.

At day break she jumped out of the hole
to find the way she had lost
suddenly a helicopter then hovered over
and she waved her hands and jumped all over with joy.

She was rescued and a happy ending it was
but it is's not always so with every soul
one's fate hangs between life and death
to be lost in the woods is no joke!

Those were the days

Old Age

Grey and bald
wrinkled face
tummy out
uneven gait.

Slipping into old age
slumped in a corner
dusk overtakes
no limelight no centerstage.

A smile may drop
though rarely
to disappear soon
without a trace.

It feels no good
to swallow bitter pills
but what else one can do
in old age!

Those were the days

Meaningful Goals

It's not easy to know
what shall work and what shall not
but patience and persistence help
to overcome all odds.

The problem is not with the goals
but with the effort put in and the approach
and direction taken to reach the goal.

It's better to plan and prepare well
and to listen to the old age advice and experience,
for how one starts it matters a lot
the initial advantage that it gives
and to save the effort for the final shot.

The goals that one sets define the purpose
and give meaning to what one does
difficulties come but one gets the strength
to face them and not to give up hope!

To Close The Distance

Why raise our voice
when restraint works better.

Some words hurt but more their tone!

Let's make up with them whom we have hurt!

Someone who's close is also a friend
expect back nothing for friendship sake.

We need to go over what all has passed
to know know whether and where we have hurt others
and slept over it.

Those were the days

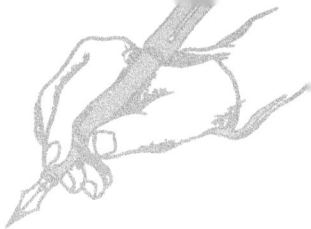

There's no need to wait any longer
but to take some steps
to break the ice
and to learn from that experience.

Whom we have missed
when they went into a shell,
we must go forward
and bring them back.

They shall also realize and understand too
when we approach them as a friend,
and no longer would they remain strangers again
whom we knew and who know us well!

Vinod Khurana

Silence and Speech

Everything has a voice
but no need for an audience.

We who speak much miss all what they say
we want to be heard while silent they remain.

How in the world the two shall meet
the silence and speech!

Until they come together
the nature and human being
the things will remain the same as they have been.

Nature is the same as it has been
man has to keep aside
his selfishness and greed.

To woo the purity of silence
and leave the pomp of make believe!

Those were the days

Childhood and Old Age

The childhood memories
the longest they stay
and give company to souls
withered with age.

The life passes
in accumulating things
which give no pleasure,
as does a smile,
a few good words
and a little care.

But who has the time
for the slow and old!

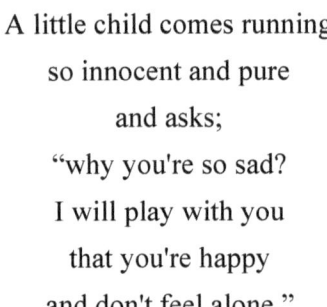

A little child comes running
so innocent and pure
and asks;
"why you're so sad?
I will play with you
that you're happy
and don't feel alone."

What the child feels
why the grown ups don't
what should come naturally
why that's ignored.

Wiser in old age
but why grown ups don't learn!

Those were the days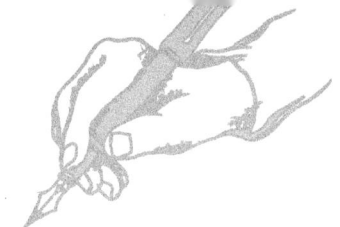

What We Hear and See

Did we see what passed before our eyes
and hear what was so close to our ears!

Many things we don't hear and see
the reality is larger than we think.

It's's good we're ignorant of some things
but there're some things we shouldn't miss!

Every specie is made differently!

What's given to one
others don't have it.

And moreover he has made us so
that we may seek and touch
the realms beyond our reach!

We trust what we hear and see
but each soul is unique
extending its scope of reality.

And that's the beauty
we 're more than we think!

Those were the days

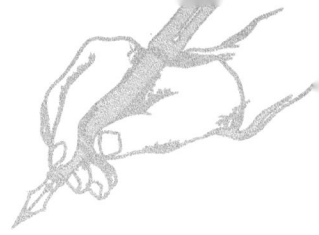

What Happens

Some say nothing happens
some say much is happening
how we view things it makes a difference.

To see more of what can be seen
and to do more of what can be done
that matters
to make the world move.

Two steps forward one step back
still the world moves ahead

They're no less powerful who push it back
more hands are needed
that it doesn't go back.

And a mighty pull
to cover more steps
not to leave behind
who can't keep in step
to lift them or hold their hand.

A lot depends upon how we act!

The choice is ours
to raise the world
or make it worse.

There's none to help
but we ourselves!

Those were the days

Do or Die

There's no easy way out
no short cut
no time to wait
but to take the plunge
to do or die
or to watch and wait
and die anyway.

"Work is worship"
not hope and wishes
God is with the doers
in every specie.

To command is easy
to serve difficult
difficulties multiply for them
who take it easy.

The world needs doers
no magic no soothsayers.

Who earn their bread
they're blessed,
and who share their bread
wear a crown on their head,
not seen by man
but by the kings in heaven!

Those were the days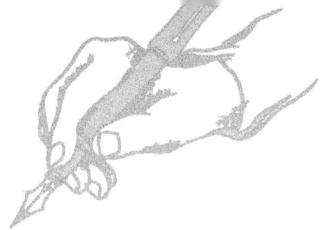

Friends or Family

Friends or family whom to choose!

Duty or freedom
never come alone.

One spends all the time as one wants
yet goes on complaining ever,
the other steals a few moments
to get over their pain.

Both keep the flock together
but in different ways.

One nurtures life
the other gives life to life,
one binds in chains
the other breaks them away.

Life's full of twists and unexpected turns
and who will stand by us in need
but the family and our friends.

Life goes on one way or the other
a family we raise to call our own
but with friends one never feels alone!

Those Early Days

Partition made them refugees
as they crossed over to the other side,
a little girl could not understand this
why they had to flee leaving everything behind.

One room they occupied in an old house
the other rooms were occupied by others similarly placed,
the house lay abandoned by its earlier occupants
who crossed over to the opposite side.

There she stayed for twenty years
studied, grew up and married there
and then the family migrated
to far west.

Now a grandmother herself
she could never forget those days
and came looking for the house
passing through lanes and by lanes.

Everything there had changed
but to her they appeared the same,
the school(now dilapitated)where she studied,
the ground(now a dump yard)where they played,
the well(now dry) from where they used to fetch water,
and the tree (now in the midst of a road crossing) where
they used to hang a swing.

Relieved to find her original base
on which so much was later laid,
nothing pleased her as much
as those childhood days.

Such is the book of life
imprints on which fade as we age,
but the first impressions are so deep
they remain even when dementia sets in at old age.

The old memories are revived,
the latter ones make no sense whatsoever,
as if there's nothing there worth to remember
to match those early days!

Those were the days

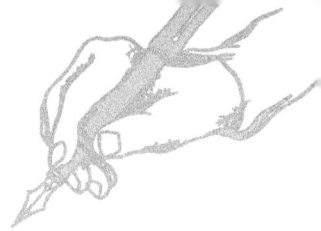

To Run After Things

Wheels under the feet
or flat footed,
to circle the globe
or to turn on one's feet,
isn't it the same thing!

When the heart is in place
and the world under our feet,
we run after things,
but what we have with us
it's way above everything!

What's Worship

God in man it's alright
but to call a man God
can we digest this!

To worship a form or formlessness
it's alright,
but to worship a human form
can we accept this!

Why one leaves behind all his mind and knowledge
and believes blindly!

Those were the days

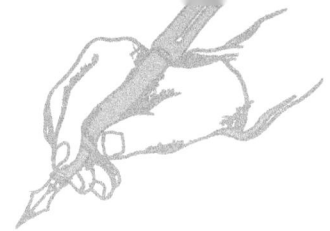

To follow a crowd
praising the Lord
no harm in it.

But when man becomes God
to worship him in place of God
is there any spirituality in it!

To do one's best
with a pure heart and mind,
that's enough
and the best form of worship.

Vinod Khurana

Home

Home is where the children grow,
the parents struggle
to make them comfortable,
sacrificing their own needs and comforts;
showering their love and blessings
with a prayer on their lips.

That the children progress and touch every height,
but at the same time at heart they remain simple and humble.

Those were the days

They let them leave to pursue what they wish,
and left alone they count everyday
to hear from them that they're doing fine
and whether they need anything.

The children understand that it's not so easy
and then struggle to stand on their own feet,
and in course of time when they become parents
they do all what their parents did!

Vinod Khurana

Song of Nature

Who have no mind
and no time,
for the pretty flowers
and the song of birds,
the trees around
and the flowing river,
how can they find happiness
being blind to its source!

And the one with no worries and cares
has friends among flowers and birds,
the trees around and the flowing river,
happy and contented at all times,
with nothing with them
they live a fuller life.

Those were the days

Things don't matter in life
but being alive to the nature's gifts,
how much happiness do they bring,
and the way the soul soars and sings.

What more in life do we need!

Blind Faith

What is given
we don't see,
and that which is hidden
we run after it.

What do we get
only disappointment and misery.

When we appreciate what is given
and go deep into it,
we find more of that
which is hidden from us.

Those were the days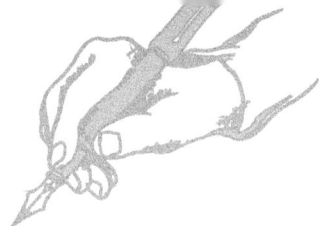

And as we go deeper and deeper
it connects us with the unknown
but a little differently;
than those who live by blind faith only.

Irrespective of what they see or don't see
and stay ignorant of many things.

Vinod Khurana

Not Someone Else

Looking back in time
there're things
we feel we shouldn't have done,
had we not done them
we would have been someone else,
who we don't know.

When we look ahead in time
we want to be someone else
whom we adore,
but whom we don't know.

If we remain who we're
and do all that what we can,
and a little more of
what we're best at,
we reach there as we can be
and not as someone else.

Those were the days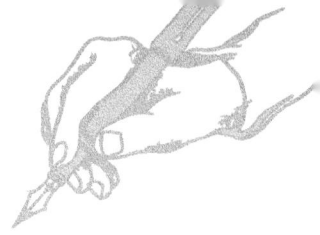

To Be Watchful

To err is human
to admit it is human
and to apologize for it is human,
but how many do it.

Humanity has variations
from sub human to divine
the choice is so wide,
to move up or compromise.

What's the way out
to be watchful at any cost
for a faulty step it takes
to lose it all!

Vinod Khurana

Gift of Love

Gift of love,
a kind word,
or a silent prayer
the more one gives
the more one gets
and it costs nothing;
but there's dearth of it
and that's the tragedy.

The world's after material gifts
but where's the love in it,
and where there'e love
the gift's an offering
no give and take in it.

Those were the days

Battlefield of Mind

One side the wise
the crooked on the other side
in between the multitude
pulled on either side.

To tilt towards the wise
or be snared by the opposite side,
the battle goes on
in the battlefield of mind.

Warriors switch places
confusing the common mind
which side is stronger
it's not easy to decide!

Vinod Khurana

Make Me Whatever

Make me not famous
but grant me the vision
to see what I see
and that too what I don't.

Whether or not I perform some big task
But enable me as much
that I may lift the weary souls
and mend the broken hearts.

The world may listen or not
But give me strength and resolve
to make the world a better place
while I live and last.

Those were the days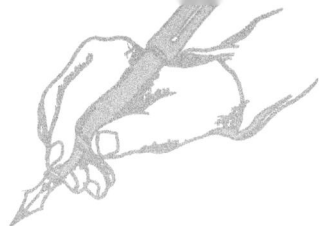

Every step of mine's under your watch
And also what I think and my thoughts
Pray hold my hand that I do what I ought
lest I go astray and in in a bind I am caught.

Make me whatever that be
whether or not it carries any position or rank
but give me enough wisdom I pray
to discern right from wrong!

My Dream

When I was young
my dream was my world
me at the center
nothing mattered much.

Then I went out
all on my own
I was rubbed and jostled
and tossed all over.

Those were the days

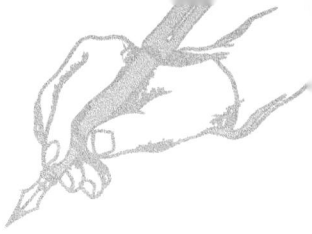

I struggled and gasped
with not a straw to hold
how could I breathe
my dream was on hold.

Now that I am done with
and have no ambition or steam
my dream has remained a dream
nothing more and with no change in it!

Cry For Help

Mend the crack
join the tear
eyes with tears
need a shoulder and an ear.

Every cry calls
most hear it not
some hear and ignore
and don't do what they ought.

But one's not enough there so much pain in the world
it's a matter of time and luck
lend a hand while one can
for next it could be anyone's turn.

Those were the days

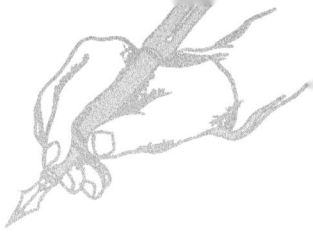

Help Yourself

There are some who are made of steel
they neither cry nor weep
and come out of adversity
stronger in spirit.

Then there're some compassionate spirits
who help everyone and whoever they meet
thus fulfilling themselves and also their need
the world stands firm because of such spirits.

When you help others you help yourself
when you join the fissures you build yourself
and when you make tears turn into a smile
you truly raise yourself!

Vinod Khurana

Sing a Song

Drag me not into
what's right or wrong
I want to be myself
and sing a song.

Where was I
me and my song
which I sang to myself
before I was born.

Let me recall
what was that song
that I have not yet sung since I was born
to my Love who has waited long.

Those were the days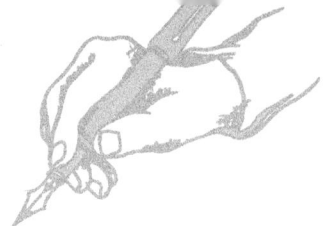

Within I feel incomplete
I spit venom and make no music
but into my heart when I delve deep
I find my Love who was always with me.

Nothing matters what we call right or wrong
we carry ourselves and our songs
into that abode far and beyond
where even deep silence sings million songs!

Thoughts

If nothing comes to mind
one's not thinking enough
and why think a thought
that inspires none.

A thought well thought
when it's given shape
such impact it makes
that's lasting and great.

They make or break
the thoughts you entertain
but both make history
one to love and the other to hate.

Those were the days

Think the unthinkable
that's not yet thought
and let there be novelty
in every step you walk.

Woo also those thoughts
that weigh heavy on your heart
hard lessons they teach
that you'll remember always.

Thoughts are thoughts
they occupy you much
but there's work to do
let the thoughts wait!

Vinod Khurana

Sow Such Deeds

Beauty is in flowers
but it disappears soon
a good turn comes
but is overtaken soon.

Let there be beauty
in whatever you do
and stand like a rock
in adversity and misfortune.

Better it be short
but meaningful
than to live long
empty and remorseful.

Say it with flowers
and walk on green grass
but sow such deeds
that even nature envies thee!

Those were the days

Imagination

Rusted imagination
it doesn't work
and pettiness rules
with heart shut.

Open up and soften your heart
to think and feel much
to look around and everywhere
into depths below and higher up.

Free the imagination of its yoke
and imagine new things
stretch your imagination as far
that it crosses every limit.

What one imagines
he lives in dreams
and one who gives them shape
he lives his dreams!

Nakedness

What's there to show
but our nakedness
and as we cover
more we show.

Add value
to this clay mold
that our nakedness
becomes not an eyesore.

Those were the days

Round and shapely
that's common lore
a bubbling volcano
it spits out gold.

Naked's the truth
shed your false robes
and inspire millions
with the nakedness that shows!

A Thief

Money and wealth
what's there to steal
poor have nothing
yet some steal their two meals.

Give credit where due
and respect one's feelings
even a thief's richer
by what he steals.

Who plans by night
and feigns ignorance
in day time
his intention's not right.

Those were the days

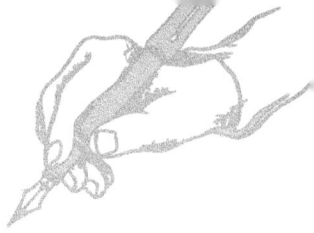

Means are important
they meet a good end
but when end's everything
there's no rest and peace.

A thief's no thief
who makes his two ends meet
but what steals one's conscience
a thief it's indeed!

Vinod Khurana

Introspection

Noise's noise
no music it makes
those who dare
history they make.

Blame none
and learn from everyone
weigh your words
lest they hurt someone.

Fools they are
who refuse to learn
but warn them still
they may break the habit.

Friends are friends
heed their advice
it's well thought of
soon you shall realize!

Those were the days

Change The Change

What there is
one doesn't see
and when entangled
he suspects everything.

The wise know
and see everything
but open not their mouth
till some are ready.

When times change
from bad to worse
and decline is steep
even the hope sinks.

Someone raises his head
to arrest the trend
and those who lie low
now see some hope.

Invite not the doom
and give up so soon
change the change
and turn it your way.

Time's now ripe
tarry not awhile
the choice's between
do or die!

Those were the days

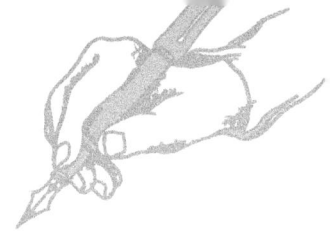

Prince of Hearts

This get together's so very different
spring in march with fragrance different
the prince of hearts fills that lacks in everything
with love and wisdom that transcends distance however
far that may be.

He's special and so very different
whatever he does it makes a difference
what's that difference that makes no difference
the different shades of a color will make hardly any
difference.

One who thinks over what all he sees
and gives meaning to every little thing
in his own way that's so different and unique
and this makes him a darling of everyone who lives.

Vinod Khurana

It's a privilege to spend a few moments with him
we have seen him grow so wholesome and fully
and what a pleasure it's to raise a toast with him
this's an opportunity of lifetime which none should miss.

Come all from all corners whatever the constraints be
Blessed's the prince and who all party with him
these words I don't write they flow automatically
such's his presence that thoughts mold into poetry!

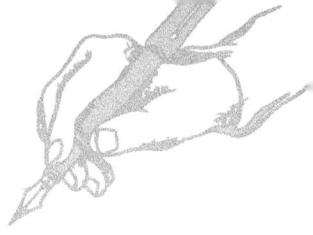

Hope

Take the wind out
lest the balloon bursts
or prick it early
before the pressure builds up.

Give in a little to him
who doesn't listen
but fear him whose mind's made up
he wants your scalp and's always dangerous.

When one's much adored
his indiscretion's not ignored
the ground he lost is lost
he's not invincible any more.

He's to tread with caution
and watch his word and its tone
what came to him of its own
he has to struggle to make it his own.

Hope hopes against hope
that the best will come back soon
riding on the very shoulders
that earlier gave up so soon!

Those were the days

Politics

If you are
what others think
transparent you are
with no secret.

When in politics
reveal not your cards
play them one by one
the trump card at the last.

When you play with swords
you hurt each other
and when feelings are hurt
that's more dangerous.

Say not that you reform
the politics at play
when people see through your game
and with what authority can you usher any change.

It's not you but the people who make
what you're and their own fate
but when they believe in what you say
in good faith they entrust to you even their own fate.

Politics is both meaningful and desirable
when people come before individuals
but when individuals advance their own interest
politics and principles part ways.

Those were the days

Walls Hear

Walls hear
the silent whisper
nothing's private
nor a secret.

What to do
when to do
one needs to ask
how to do.

Black and white
we mix the two
but the wise pick
nothing but true.

Ambition blinds
one soares high
but when the wind's contrary
it beats him left and right.

Nothing's your own
not even your soul
that goes back there
from where it was loaned.

Lead not anyone
but your own self
when others feel inspired
the world shall change itself !

Those were the days

Why Sell Everything

Who's not with him
he's against him
and who's with him
let him be as he's.

What he says it sells
what doesn't sell
he doesn't keep with him
may that be his own belief.

Whatever there's
it has to change
what bears his stamp
only that can stay.

He sacrificed everything
even his heart and soul
so that they're happy
his methods who support.

Vinod Khurana

Nothing matters
but power and position
that he thinks he has seen
and now firmly believes.

He says he'll deliver
and shall not leave
whoever's a stickler
let him better leave!

But what sells that's not everything
and what doesn't sell it stays with us
and it will carry us through thick and thin,
but when everything's sold by the seller he has nothing
left with him.

Those were the days

House on Fire

No fire no fireballs
just a light snowfall
no heat no warmth
but a pleasant rainfall.

This is my field so he says
and I am the lord
till my land
but only as a tenant.

I look away
and don't care
sow as you like
but grow grain good and fine.

Vinod Khurana

A sermon they give
that's all
anything I do
they find fault.

No place is there
for such die hards
they are laid low
a good riddance.

I am clean
with no personal agenda
and all I do
it's only dharma.

Teach me not
right or wrong
I am a saint
who can do no wrong.

Those were the days

Politics is my way
and I give shape
to what is good
so why question my ways!

It's not your field
even you're on mortgage
he'll extract the rent with penalty
who make the tiller a tenant.

Play no politics with him
who can checkmate you anytime
Your house's on fire and you have no choice
seek his forgiveness for harsher could be his sentence.

We have to pay the price for our transgressions
and none can go scot free
But he's merciful
seek his mercy for acts done even unknowingly.

Vinod Khurana

Thorns and Friends

Let me walk
over the thorns
that are laid in my path.

A flower smiles
among the thorns
which I woo to kiss the flower.

You walk with me
over the thorns
my true friends you really are

Lift me not
who walk with me
lest I forget how sore are your feet.

Those were the days

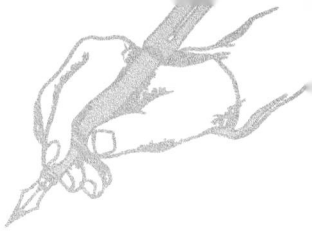

I walked I listened
a leader you made me
but why I now abhor you who were dear to me.

Their words are bitter
like an ugly spat
and I am at peace without them.

A good counselor is your best friend
heed him and all shall be well
and beware of the fairweather friends!

Vinod Khurana

A House Divided

A house stands
on strong foundation
but it crumbles
when abandoned.

When foundation shakes
can it withstand a quake
one who lives in it
is he safe.

When a brother is estranged
the house disintegrates
and when he talks sense
why should communication break.

Those were the days

One may stand taller
and raise his stake
but even a small compromise
may prove costly on the way.

The house has been built
brick by brick
each brick well washed
no filth in between.

The sane voice be heard
though it may pinch
and let the house stand
strong and majestic.

Light shines
but for a while
some wake up and arise
and some are happy to draw the blinds!

www.ingramcontent.com/pod-product-compliance
Lightning Source LLC
LaVergne TN
LVHW061550070526
838199LV00077B/6976